Editor
Sara Connolly

Illustrator
The Development Source

Cover Artist
Brenda DiAntonis

Editor in Chief
Ina Massler Levin, M.A.

Creative Director
Karen J. Goldfluss, M.S. Ed.

Art Production Manager
Kevin Barnes

Art Coordinator
Renée Christine Yates

Imaging
Leonard P. Swierski
Nathan P. Rivera

Publisher

Mary D. Smith, M.S. Ed.

Grades
3-4

Act FLUENCY

- Helps Build Confident Readers
- Improves Oral Reading Skills
- Introduces a Variety of Reading Materials

Number of Syllables

horse	1
village	2
harness	2

multicolored

Author

Melissa Hart, M.F.A.

Teacher Created Resources, Inc.
12621 Western Avenue
Garden Grove, CA 92841
www.teachercreated.com

ISBN: 978-1-4206-8051-5

©2008 Teacher Created Resources, Inc.
Reprinted, 2019
Made in U.S.A.

Teacher Created Resources

Table of Contents

Introduction

A fluent child is an empowered child. Fluency implies much more than simply being able to read a piece of writing. Fluent students articulate with confidence; their words are clear and their voices are well-modulated. Fluent readers demonstrate not just reading skills but the ability to understand and make meaning of a written piece for both themselves and listeners.

Each section of *Activities for Fluency* has been designed with this goal in mind—-to create active, enthusiastic readers who know how to bring a piece of writing to life. In a 2002 interview with the former U.S. Assistant Secretary of the Office of Elementary and Secondary Education, Illinois reading expert Dr. Eunice Greer noted that fluency is the most neglected element of early reading instruction. "When kids can read rapidly and accurately," Dr. Greer explained, "what this does is this frees up their little brains so that they can attend to what the text is about, they can attend to meaning."

Activities for Fluency incorporates meaningful and exciting pieces across genres; it includes poetry, historical fiction, non-fiction, fables, Reader's Theater, and short stories. Teachers are encouraged to read each piece aloud, modeling skillful fluency techniques for students. In addition, students may read along with the teacher, copying pacing, tone, and inflection. Within each section, students explore vocabulary words and their meanings, and examine parts of speech and punctuation. They learn literary concepts such as figurative language, characterization and setting. They also learn to read aloud effectively, with emotion and inflection.

Each section of this book culminates in a Fluency Report Card which asks students to read a piece aloud to their teacher. The student receives feedback on key elements of fluency, including rate of reading, accuracy of word pronunciation, and tone. One part of the rubric allows teachers to note what students did best in their reading, whether in terms of poise and presentation, or simply in demonstrating the confidence to read an entire piece aloud.

As students move through grammar school to high school and college, they meet with countless opportunities to demonstrate fluency. Students are asked to read aloud in class, give speeches, participate in debates, and perform in plays. *Activities for Fluency* will help to develop skillful habits and techniques so that students can move through the educational system with self-assurance and success.

How to Use This Book

Activities for Fluency (Grades 3–4) offers students a variety of methods by which to become fluent, confident readers. Each section begins with a written piece: non-fiction, short fiction, scripts, songs, poems, and riddles. Activities follow, each designed to familiarize readers with unfamiliar words and punctuation marks in each piece. In addition, students will become familiar with stressed and unstressed syllables, breathing patterns in reading aloud, suffixes, prefixes, and root words, inflection, and reading with emotion. A fluency report card follows each section, designed to evaluate students' rate of reading, accuracy, and prosody—that is, pitch, volume, and rhythm when reading aloud.

Model the reading of each piece aloud before beginning the accompanying activities. Then, ask students to read along with you, mimicking your own reading rate and prosody. Next, invite students to complete the activities following each piece. These range from crossword puzzles and word searches to question and answer sections, flash cards, bingo, and classroom games. When you are confident that students can read a piece aloud fluently, evaluate them with the report card provided. A final section on the report card allows you to evaluate each student's particular strength in reading aloud.

As you work through the book, consider using these techniques:

- Peer Readers—Match a fluent reader up with a student whose skills are still developing. Ask each pair to work together, reading each piece aloud and completing the exercises.

- Group Collaboration—Many of these pieces are already in Readers' Theater format. Others are well-known songs or poems. Ask students to perform pieces in front of the class, to build familiarity with language, inflection, and characterization.

- Bingo Cards—Several sections of this book include Bingo cards. Consider mixing up cards from numerous pieces, and using a variety of vocabulary words as students play.

- Flash Cards—Likewise, many sections of this book include flash cards with pictures on one side, and words on the other. Consider cutting out flash cards and creating a master deck with which students can practice all of the vocabulary words in this book. They may use the cards to help memorize pronunciation and spelling, and they may also use them to form sentences. Humor works well with this age group—challenge students to create funny phrases with their flash cards.

How to Use This Book *(cont.)*

In addition, consider the following techniques for teaching vocabulary and fluency:

- Ask students to work in groups to create an illustrated book of the vocabulary words and their meanings.

- Play "Guess the Definition." One student writes down the correct definition of the vocabulary word. The others write down false definitions, close enough to the original definition that their classmates might be fooled. Read all definitions, and then challenge students to guess the correct one. The students whose definitions mislead their classmates get a point for each student fooled.

- Use the word in five different sentences. Compare sentences and discuss.

- Write a short story using as many of the words as possible. Students may then read their stories in groups.

- Encourage your students to use each new vocabulary word in a conversation five times during one day. They can take notes on how and when the word was used, and then share their experience with the class.

- Play "Vocabulary Charades." Each student or group of students gets a word to act out. Other students must guess the word.

- Play "Vocabulary Pictures." Each student or group of students must draw a picture representing a word on the chalkboard or on paper. Other students must guess the word.

- Challenge students to a Vocabulary Bee. In groups or separately, students must spell the word correctly, and give its proper definition.

Fluency is much more than reading a passage without mistakes. We hope that this book will encourage your students to personalize their reading through thoughtful pacing, inventive performance techniques, and creative methods of making each piece of writing their own.

Standards

Each lesson in *Activities for Fluency*, Grades 3–4, meets one or more of the following standards, which are used with permission from McREL (Copyright 2007, McREL, Mid-continent Research for Education and Learning. Telephone: 303/337-0990. Website: www.mcrel.org .)

Language Arts Standards	Page Number
Uses strategies to write for a variety of purposes	13, 52, 68, 82, 99, 107, 131, 134
Writes expository compositions	14
Writes narrative accounts	38
Writes autobiographical compositions	29
Writes in response to literature	81, 89, 113
Writes personal letters	110
Uses grammatical and mechanical conventions in written compositions	74, 83, 84, 85, 98, 121, 122
Use a variety of context clues to decode unknown words	9, 10, 11, 12, 17, 18-21, 22, 33, 41, 49, 50, 55-60, 65-67, 91-94, 97, 100-101, 105, 114, 116, 123, 129, 130
Understands level-appropriate reading vocabulary	9, 17, 25, 26, 33, 41, 49, 50, 28, 51, 73, 78, 86, 106, 125, 132, 133
Monitors own reading strategies and makes modifications as needed. Adjusts speed of reading to suit purpose and difficulty of the material	8, 15, 16, 23, 24, 31, 32, 39, 40, 47, 48, 55, 56, 63, 64, 71, 72, 79, 80, 87, 88, 95, 96, 103, 104, 111, 112, 119, 120, 127, 128, 135, 136, 137
Uses reading skills and strategies to understand a variety of literary passages and texts.	8, 15, 16, 23, 24, 30, 31, 32, 39, 40, 47, 48, 55, 56, 63, 64, 71, 72, 79, 80, 87, 88, 95, 96, 103, 104, 111, 112, 115, 119, 120, 127, 128, 135, 136, 137
Understands the ways in which language is used in literary texts	35-37, 42-46,
Knows the defining characteristics of a variety of informational texts	8, 16, 25, 32, 40, 48, 56, 64, 72, 80, 88, 96, 104, 112, 120, 128, 136
Understands structural patterns or organization in informational texts	90, 124
Makes basic oral presentations to class	70, 118
Uses a variety of verbal communication skills	53, 54, 69, 76, 102, 108, 117, 126, 109

Sample Fluency Report Card

Directions: Students will be asked to read a piece of writing from each section out loud. Using a stopwatch, time your students' reading.

Together, fill out the Fluency Report Card similar to the sample below.

Rate of Reading	Minutes Seconds 2 36
Accuracy	Number of Mistakes *2 mistakes*
Tone	Pitch, Volume, and Rhythm *Pitch was a little high, but volume was perfect. Focus on varying your rhythm as you read, so as not to sound robotic. Practice challenging words including "castle," and "breathe."*
What You Did Best	Your strengths in fluency! *Your pronunciation is excellent, Jim. Your volume is pleasant to hear—not too loud, and not too soft. Well done!*

*Note to Teacher

Rate of Reading: Student should read at a pleasant, conversational pace, not too slowly, and not too quickly.

Accuracy: Student should read with a minimum of mistakes in pronunciation and pauses for punctuation.

Tone: Student should read at a pleasant pitch, with moderate volume, and should vary rhythm as appropriate to each sentence.

Earthquake!

Hurry! Get under a table or desk. The ground is shaking! There must be an earthquake.

The Earth's crust is made up of plates. When these plates move, an earthquake happens. Many parts of the world have earthquakes quite often. They can be small, and people hardly notice them. Other times, earthquakes can be very large.

We measure quakes using a system called a "Richter scale." An earthquake which measures 2.0 is very small. An earthquake that measures 6.0 will uproot trees and damage buildings.

You can protect yourself during an earthquake. As soon as you feel the ground begin to shake, get under a sturdy object such as a desk or table. Cover your head and neck with your arms. If you are outside, go to open area. Stay away from trees and power lines.

Remain calm. Earthquakes may be scary, but they do not last long!

Flash Cards

Note to Teacher: Make double-sided copies, aligning words with the correct pictures so that they appear front-to-back.

Directions: Cut out these flash cards on the lines. Use them to practice spelling and fluency.

earthquake	table
buildings	Earth
cover	plates
uproot	power lines

Flash Cards *(cont.)*

Fill in the Blank

Directions: Fill in the blanks to complete the sentences below, using words from the Word Bank below. You will not use all of the words in the Bank.

1. An earthquake happens when the Earth's _____ move.

2. A large earthquake can damage _____ .

3. _____ your neck and head during an earthquake.

4. An _____ can uproot trees.

5. If you are inside, get under a _____ when the ground starts to shake.

6. If you are outside during an earthquake, stay away from _____ .

Word Bank	
measure	table
outside	buildings
plates	power lines
earthquake	cover

Write the Word

Directions: Write the word below the picture.

Caption the Picture

Directions: Look at the scene below. On the blank lines, write a one sentence caption that explains each picture. Use the following vocabulary words in your captions: cover, table, power lines, uproot, buildings.

During an Earthquake

Directions: Some parts of the world do not get many earthquakes. Imagine that your friend is visiting California, which gets many earthquakes. Explain to your friend what to do in an earthquake.

Use the words from the Word Bank below in your explanation.

Word Bank	
desk	earthquake
table	outside
power lines	trees
buildings	cover

Fluency Report Card

Directions: Read the story out loud to your teacher. Ask your teacher to time your reading with a watch.

Together, fill out the chart below.

Rate of Reading	Minutes Seconds
Accuracy	Number of Mistakes
Tone	Pitch, Volume, and Rhythm
What You Did Best	Your strengths in fluency!

Beluga Whales

Visit the Vancouver Aquarium in Canada, and you will see white whales. Beluga whales are small. They breathe through a blowhole. They have stout bodies and small heads. The name "Beluga" means "white one" in Russian.

These whales live in the cold Arctic ocean. They swim down to warm water during the summer. They swim slowly. They dive for squid and fish.

Some people call this whale a "sea canary." This is because Belugas make a lot of noise. They click, whistle, and chatter. This allows them to talk with each other.

These whales are friendly. They travel in pods—groups of whales. They hunt together. Sometimes, one pod joins another. Large pods include 10,000 whales.

Beluga whales are fun to watch. See them if you can!

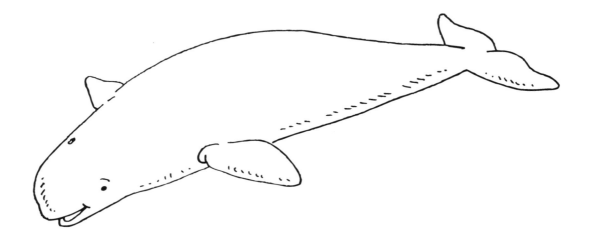

Picture Words

Directions: Study the words below the pictures. Say them out loud with your teacher. Then, say them out loud by yourself.

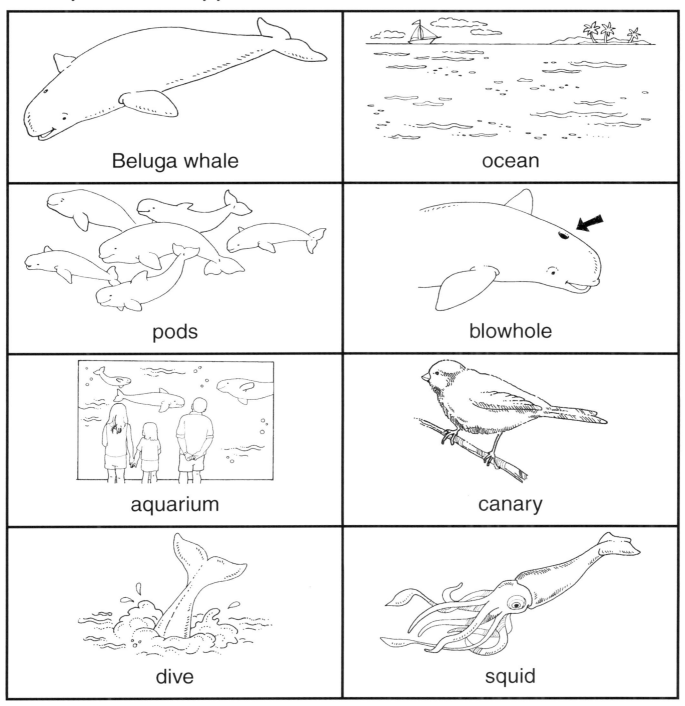

Beluga whale	ocean
pods	blowhole
aquarium	canary
dive	squid

Beluga Bingo

Directions: Play Bingo, using words from "Beluga Whales."

Copy the words below onto individual file cards or small pieces of paper. Choose one person to be the Caller. The Caller begins by choosing one word to call out. Each player then marks the square on his or her game card which contains that word.

Players may use markers in the form of dried beans, pennies, or small pebbles. You may want to play so that the first person to mark off an entire row across, down, or diagonally wins. Alternatively, you might want to play until every word has been called and marked.

Beluga whale	canary	fish
squid	blowhole	ocean
dive	aquarium	pods

Beluga Bingo *(cont.)*

pods	squid	blowhole
canary	fish	aquarium
ocean	dive	Beluga whale

Beluga Bingo *(cont.)*

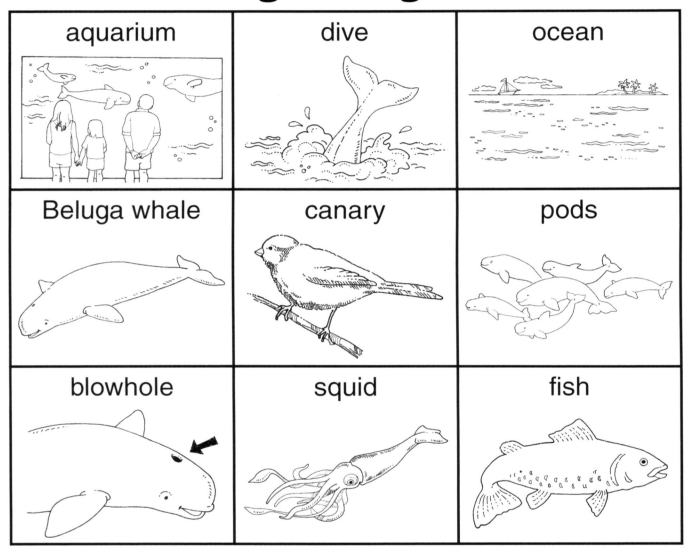

aquarium	dive	ocean
Beluga whale	canary	pods
blowhole	squid	fish

Beluga Bingo *(cont.)*

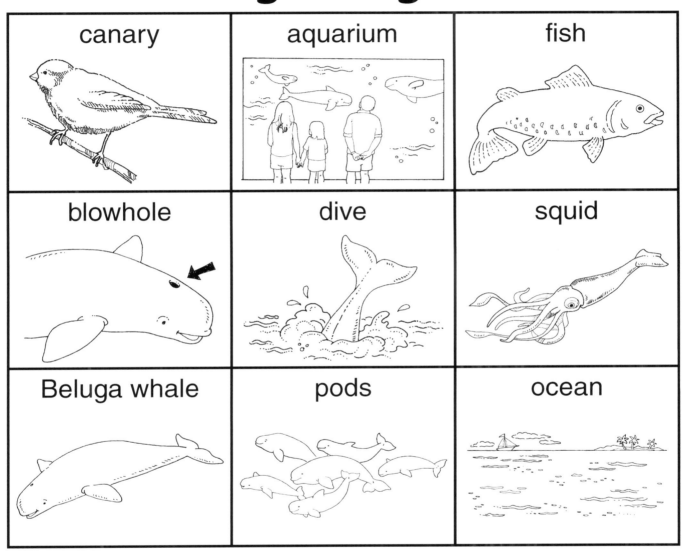

| canary | aquarium | fish |
| squid | | |

Which Word?

Directions: Below, circle the correct word in each pair to complete the sentence. Then, write the word in the blank.

1. You can see a Beluga in an _____ .

        blowhole   aquarium

2. Pods travel together in the _____ .

         squid   ocean

3. Belugas eat _____ and fish.

     pods   squid

4. The whale breathes through a _____ .

        dive   blowhole

5. "Sea _____ " is another name for a Beluga.

   fish   canary

6. The _____ is noisy and likes to travel with others.

   canary   Beluga whale

Fluency Report Card

Directions: Read the story out loud to your teacher. Ask your teacher to time your reading with a watch.

Together, fill out the chart below.

Rate of Reading	Minutes Seconds
Accuracy	Number of Mistakes
Tone	Pitch, Volume, and Rhythm
What You Did Best	Your strengths in fluency!

Hot Air Balloons

Have you ever seen a hot air balloon in flight? It is beautiful! The balloon has bright colors. Ropes attach it to a basket. You can ride in the basket. Some baskets can hold ten people!

Two French brothers invented the hot air balloon in 1783. They sent a duck, a sheep, and a rooster up in a basket first. Later, people began to ride in hot air balloons.

Today, propane powers balloons. The tank rides in the basket. Air heated by a flame inflates the balloon. This makes it lighter than outside air. Then, the balloon can rise and float on the wind.

Take a ride in a hot air balloon if you have a chance. It is a very peaceful, yet exciting, adventure!

Parts of a Balloon

Directions: Color the balloon below. Then, label the parts of the balloon on the lines given, using words from the article on the previous page.

Flash Cards

Note to Teacher: Make double-sided copies, aligning words with the correct pictures so that they appear front-to-back.

Directions: Cut out these flash cards on the lines. Use them to practice spelling and fluency.

balloon	basket
rooster	brothers
propane	flame
people	inflate

26

Flash Cards (cont.)

Crossword Puzzle

Directions: Fill in the blanks below and complete the crossword puzzle.

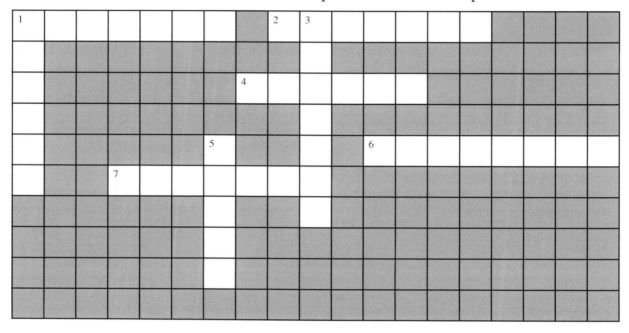

Across

1. This rises when filled with hot air.

2. This fuels a flame, making hot air to power a balloon.

4. These can be passengers in a hot air balloon.

6. From France, they invented the hot air balloon.

7. This means to fill an object with a gas such as air.

Down

1. People ride beneath the balloon in this.

3. This was one of the first passengers in a balloon.

5. This inflates a balloon, making it lighter than outside air.

Write a Diary Entry

Directions: Pretend you are the duck who first rode in a hot air balloon. Write a diary entry about your experience in the space below. Use the words from the Word Bank in your description.

Word Bank	
hot air balloon	rooster
brothers	basket
flame	wind
air	quiet

_____

_____

_____

_____

_____

_____

_____

_____

_____

_____

_____

True or False

Directions: Answer each question by circling **true** or **false**.

1. Hot air balloons sink when they are inflated.

   True   **False**

2. Balloon baskets can only hold two people.

   True   **False**

3. Riding in a hot air balloon is peaceful and exciting.

   True   **False**

4. Ropes attach the hot air balloon to the basket.

   True   **False**

5. Two French brothers were the first balloon passengers.

   True   **False**

6. A propane flame inflates the basket of a hot air balloon.

   True   **False**

Fluency Report Card

Directions: Read the article out loud to your teacher. Ask your teacher to time your reading with a watch.

Together, fill out the chart below.

Rate of Reading	Minutes Seconds
Accuracy	Number of Mistakes
Tone	Pitch, Volume, and Rhythm
What You Did Best	Your strengths in fluency!

Stopping by Woods on a Snowy Evening

by Robert Frost

Robert Frost was a poet who loved to write about the people and landscapes of New England.

Whose woods these are I think I know.
His house is in the village, though;
He will not see me stopping here
To watch his woods fill up with snow.

My little horse must think it's queer
To stop without a farmhouse near
Between the woods and frozen lake
The darkest evening of the year.

He gives his harness bells a shake
To ask if there is some mistake.
The only other sound's the sweep
Of easy wind and downy flake.

The woods are lovely, dark, and deep,
But I have promises to keep,
And miles to go before I sleep,
And miles to go before I sleep.

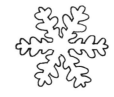

Write the Word

Directions: Study the pictures below. Then, write the correct word from the Word Bank below each picture.

1. _____	**2.** _____
3. _____	**4.** _____
5. _____	**6.** _____
7. _____	**8.** _____

Word Bank	
horse	farmhouse
village	snow
harness	snowflake
woods	evening

Syllables

A syllable is one unit of spoken language. Some words have one syllable, such as *his* or *to*. Other words have two syllables, such as *harness* (har-ness) or *farmhouse* (farm-house). Some words have three syllables, such as *promises* (prom-i-ses).

Directions: Study the words below. Count how many syllables are in each word. Write the correct number in the space provided.

The first one has been done for you.

Word	Number of Syllables
1. horse	one
2. village	
3. woods	
4. harness	
5. evening	
6. it's	

Stressed or Unstressed?

Syllables are either stressed or unstressed. This gives spoken language its rhythm. You can tell which syllables are stressed and unstressed by clapping as you sing or recite a song.

Directions: Study "Stopping by Woods on a Snowy Evening" below. Stressed syllables have a ˋ over them. Unstressed syllables have a — over them. Recite the poem. Clap along, clapping loudly with stressed syllables, and very softly with unstressed syllables.

Whose woods these are I think I know.

His house is in the village, though;

He will not see me stopping here

To watch his woods fill up with snow.

My little horse must think it's queer

To stop without a farmhouse near

Between the woods and frozen lake

The darkest evening of the year.

He gives his harness bells a shake

To ask if there is some mistake.

The only other sound's the sweep

Of easy wind and downy flake.

The woods are lovely, dark, and deep,

But I have promises to keep,

And miles to go before I sleep,

And miles to go before I sleep.

Stressed Syllables

Directions: Study the words below. First, they appear complete. Then, they are broken up into syllables. Circle the **stressed** syllables. The first one has been done for you.

1. mistake   mis   (take)

2. little   lit   tle

3. village   vil   lage

4. stopping   stop   ping

5. promises   pro   mi   ses

6. downy   down   y

7. lovely   love   ly

8. before   be   fore

Unstressed Syllables

Directions: Study the words below. First, they appear complete. Then, they are broken up into syllables. Circle the **unstressed** syllables. The first one has been done for you.

1. farmhouse   farm   (house)

2. harness   har   ness

3. mistake   mis   take

4. easy   ea   sy

5. frozen   fro   zen

6. promises   pro   mi   ses

7. darkest   dark   est

8. between   be   tween

Write a Poem

Directions: Write your own four-line poem in the space below. It does not have to rhyme. When you are finished, add accent marks above each word, according to the chart at the bottom of the page.

Stressed Syllable `	Unstressed Syllable –

Fluency Report Card

Directions: Read the poem out loud to your teacher. Ask your teacher to time your reading with a watch.

Together, fill out the chart below.

Rate of Reading	Minutes Seconds
Accuracy	Number of Mistakes
Tone	Pitch, Volume, and Rhythm
What You Did Best	Your strengths in fluency!

A White Hen

By Christina Rossetti

Christina Rossetti was born in London, in 1830. She was the youngest child in a family of poets and artists.

A white hen sitting

On white eggs three:

Next, three speckled chickens

As plump as plump can be.

An owl, and a hawk,

And a bat come to see:

But chicks beneath their mother's wing

Squat safe as safe can be.

Matching

Directions: Study the pictures on the right. Study the words on the left. Draw a line from the correct picture to the correct word.

chicks	
hen	
owl	
eggs	
bat	
hawk	
Great horned owl	
Red-tailed hawk	

Rhyming Bingo

Directions: Distribute the Bingo cards on the four following pages. Select one person to read the list of words below, one at a time. Players should mark the word on their card which rhymes with each word that the reader offers. For instance, if the reader calls out "legs," players will mark the word "eggs."

Rhyming is about sound, not spelling. For instance, even though the words "hawk" and "lock" are not spelled in a similar manner, they do rhyme.

Players may use markers in the form of dried beans, pennies, or small pebbles. You may want to play so that the first person to mark off an entire row across, down, or diagonally wins. Alternatively, you might want to play until every word has been called and marked.

men	fowl	lock
kicks	sing	cat
bump	legs	sea

Rhyming Bingo *(cont.)*

eggs	hawk	bat
wing	hen	owl
chicks	three	plump

Rhyming Bingo *(cont.)*

plump	bat	hawk
hen	three	chicks
owl	wing	eggs

Rhyming Bingo *(cont.)*

chicks	owl	wing
eggs	hawk	plump
bat	three	hen

Rhyming Bingo *(cont.)*

eggs	wing	chicks
three	bat	hen
hawk	owl	plump

Fluency Report Card

Directions: Read the poem out loud to your teacher. Ask your teacher to time your reading with a watch.

Together, fill out the chart below.

Rate of Reading	Minutes Seconds
Accuracy	Number of Mistakes
Tone	Pitch, Volume, and Rhythm
What You Did Best	Your strengths in fluency!

Sing a Song of Sixpence

This is a favorite nonsense children's poem by an anonymous—unknown—author.

Sing a song of sixpence,

A pocket full of rye;

Four and twenty blackbirds

Baked in a pie!

When the pie was opened

The birds began to sing;

Was that not a dainty dish

To set before the king?

The king was in his counting-house

Counting all his money;

The queen was in the parlor,

Eating bread and honey.

The maid was in the garden,

Hanging out the clothes;

When down came a blackbird

And snapped off her nose.

Flash Cards

Note to Teacher: Make double-sided copies, aligning words with the correct pictures so that they appear front-to-back.

Directions: Cut out these flash cards on the lines. Use them to practice spelling and fluency.

maid	king
queen	nose
pie	blackbird
bread	money
clothes	garden

Flash Cards *(cont.)*

Word Search

Directions: Find the words from the Word Bank in the Word Search below. Words appear across or down. Circle the words.

Word Bank	
king	queen
maid	bread
bird	sing
money	nose
dainty	dish

k	i	n	g	b	d	i
n	i	o	s	i	n	g
b	m	s	q	r	m	d
r	a	e	u	d	o	i
e	i	d	e	n	n	s
a	d	r	e	e	e	h
d	a	i	n	t	y	e

Captions

Directions: Study the poem, "Sing a Song of Sixpence." Then, study each picture below. Using words from the Word Bank at the bottom of the page, caption each picture. You may use words more than once in different captions.

Word Bank	
king	money
maid	blackbird
queen	birds

Breathing

Fluent readers know when to take a breath as they read out loud. Try not to take a breath in the middle of a phrase. Instead, take a breath when you see a period or come to the end of a thought. This helps your reading to flow smoothly.

Directions: Below, read "Sing a Song of Sixpence." Take a breath whenever you see a smiley face.

 Sing a song of sixpence,

A pocket full of rye;

Four and twenty blackbirds

Baked in a pie!

When the pie was opened

The birds began to sing;

Was not that dainty dish

To set before the king?

The king was in his counting-house

Counting all his money;

The queen was in the parlor,

Eating bread and honey.

The maid was in the garden,

Hanging out the clothes;

When down came a blackbird

And snapped off her nose.

More on Breathing

Directions: Read the sentences below out loud. Draw a smiley face wherever you feel you should take a breath. You may draw it above, below, or next to a word. Remember not to breathe in the middle of a phrase!

1. The queen and the king like to eat pie and cookies. Sometimes they like to eat cake.

2. I love to wake up in the morning to hear the birds singing. It puts me in a happy mood.

3. Where is that blackbird going? He is flying very close to that woman's nose!

4. I love to count my quarters and dimes. Then, I take them to the store and buy candy.

5. Bees make honey. Do you like to eat your bread with honey, peanut butter, or jam?

6. When you hang your clothes on the line to dry, they smell like fresh air. But watch out for birds!

Fluency Report Card

Directions: Read the poem out loud to your teacher. Ask your teacher to time your reading with a watch.

Together, fill out the chart below.

Rate of Reading	Minutes Seconds
Accuracy	Number of Mistakes
Tone	Pitch, Volume, and Rhythm
What You Did Best	Your strengths in fluency!

Snow!

All her life, Misty had wished for snow. She looked at pictures of fluffy white snowballs in books. She gazed at images of snowmen and snow angels on TV. But Misty lived in a town where the sun always shone. "I wish it would snow," she said sadly. "But it's hopeless."

"We are lucky," said her friends. "We get to play in the sun all day. We get to have picnics in December."

But Misty opened a magazine to a picture of kids sledding down a snowy hill. "I feel unlucky," she whispered.

Misty's father understood her. He had grown up in New York state, and he remembered the joy of playing in snow. One day in January, he told Misty, "I will be gone for a day. When I return, I will have a surprise."

Misty waited for her father to return. At last, she saw his truck roll down the street. A great pile of white fluff sat in the back of his truck.

"Snow!" Misty cried with excitement.

She helped her father to shovel the snow onto the lawn. Then, her friends ran over to play. They threw snowballs and made snow angels. Misty held snow in her hand. She licked it with the tip of her tongue. "Now, I feel like the luckiest girl in the world!" she told her father.

Root Words

Think of a root word like a building block. You can add a prefix or a suffix to make a new word.

Directions: Below, study the root words from "Snow!" Say each word out loud. Then, use a dictionary to look up the definition. Write the definitions on the lines provided.

1. luck _____

_____

2. open _____

_____

3. sled _____

_____

4. play _____

_____

5. wish _____

_____

6. hope _____

_____

7. excite _____

_____

8. sad _____

_____

The Suffix

A group of letters put at the end of a root word is called a suffix. This turns the root word into a different word.

Directions: Study the root words and the suffixes below. Then, write the root and the suffix as one word, along with the definition of the new word.

Root Word	Suffix	New Word and Definition
1. luck	+ y	= _____ _____ _____
2. excite	+ ment	= _____ _____ _____
3. sad	+ ly	= _____ _____ _____
4. hope	+ less	= _____ _____ _____
5. sled	+ ding	= _____ _____ _____

Many Words

Directions: Look at the list of root words below. Then, look at the list of suffixes. You can make at least 21 new words by combining root words and suffixes!

Write your new words in the Word Bank below. You may need to add a letter or two to form your new word. The first one has been done for you.

Root Word
luck
open
sad
sled
play
hope
excite
wish

Suffix
ly
er
ful
ed
y
ment
less
ing

Word Bank

Sledding _____ _____ _____

_____ _____ _____ _____

_____ _____ _____ _____

_____ _____ _____ _____

_____ _____ _____ _____

_____

Nouns

A noun is a person, place, or thing.

Directions: Circle the nouns from "Snow!" in the Word Search, below. Words may appear up, down, diagonally, forward, and backwards. Then, label the parts of the picture on the next page.

snowball	snowman	girl
truck	book	angel
sun	tongue	sledding

l	w	r	d	n	l	w	n
g	s	k	c	u	r	t	g
l	l	a	b	w	o	n	s
r	a	s	n	n	i	n	u
i	n	n	g	d	o	l	n
g	g	u	d	w	u	b	s
o	e	e	m	n	o	d	s
r	l	a	o	o	r	a	w
s	n	n	k	l	o	n	w

Nouns *(cont.)*

Directions: Label the parts of the picture.

Building Sentences

You can build new sentences from words in "Snow!"

Directions: Study the nouns below. Then, study the root words and suffixes. Write six new sentences on the lines given. Use one noun from the list in each sentence. Combine one root word and one suffix to create a new word for each sentence.

Nouns
kids
picnic
angel
truck
magazine

Root Words
luck
play
excite
wish
sad

Suffixes
ed
ing
iest
ful
ly

Example: The playful kids went for a swim.

1. _____

2. _____

3. _____

4. _____

5. _____

6. _____

Fluency Report Card

Directions: Read the story out loud to your teacher. Ask your teacher to time your reading with a watch.

Together, fill out the chart below.

Rate of Reading	Minutes Seconds
Accuracy	Number of Mistakes
Tone	Pitch, Volume, and Rhythm
What You Did Best	Your strengths in fluency!

Horseback Riding

James reread the letter from his cousin with concern. "I would like you to visit my ranch. See you soon! From, Bill." James folded the letter. He wanted to visit, but his mind gave him a preview of what might happen.

James was afraid of horses. Bill had two. In his head, James saw himself trying to interact with the horses. "But I'm afraid they'll bite me, or throw me to the ground," he told his mother.

"Go," Mother said. "What you discover might surprise you."

So James went to the ranch. "Let me show you my horses!" said Bill. "I'll ride one, and you can ride the other."

James felt unhappy. But he walked toward a small black horse. "This is Cal," said Bill. "He is a good horse."

Slowly, James climbed into the saddle. He put his feet in the stirrups. He felt at a disadvantage since Bill was an expert rider. But Cal trotted along gently.

"You're doing fine!" Bill called.

Then, James felt overjoyed. His mother had been right. "I like horseback riding!" he told Bill with surprise.

Root Words

Directions: Below, study the root words from "Horseback Riding." Say each word out loud. Then, use a dictionary to look up the definition. Write the definitions on the lines provided.

1. read

   _____

   _____

2. view

   _____

   _____

3. act

   _____

   _____

4. cover

   _____

   _____

5. happy

   _____

   _____

6. mark

   _____

   _____

7. advantage

   _____

   _____

8. joy

   _____

   _____

Prefixes

Directions: Combine each prefix and root word to create a new word. Then, write the new word and its definition in the space provided.

Prefix	Root Word	New Word and Definition
1. re	+ read	= _____ _____ _____
2. dis	+ cover	= _____ _____ _____
3. un	+ happy	= _____ _____ _____
4. dis	+ advantage	= _____ _____ _____
5. inter	+ act	= _____ _____ _____

Fill in the Blanks

Directions: Reread the story titled "Horseback Riding." Fill in the blanks by writing the correct words from the Word Bank below.

1. James' mind gave him a _____ of what might happen if he rode a horse.

2. James felt _____ because he was afraid of horses.

3. Someone who didn't grow up with horses might feel at a _____ when visiting a ranch.

4. Bill wanted James to _____ with his black horse.

5. James had to _____ Bill's letter while he thought about what to do.

6. James felt _____ when he learned to ride a horse.

7. Mother knew that James might _____ something that would surprise him.

8. Cal was _____ because he was such a gentle horse.

Word Bank	
preview	disadvantage
reread	overjoyed
discover	remarkable
unhappy	interact

Write a Letter

Directions: Write a a letter to James giving him advice about his trip to the ranch. Use words from the Word Bank below.

Word Bank	
letter	black
James	saddle
Bill	ride
thrown	horseback
ranch	riding
horses	afraid

Emotions in Reading

You can change the way a piece of writing sounds by adjusting your voice to express various emotions.

Directions: Practice reading the sentence below out loud. Change your reading to indicate the emotion in parentheses.

1. I'm going to go horseback riding. (scared)

2. I'm going to go horseback riding. (happy)

3. I'm going to go horseback riding. (excited)

4. I'm going to go horseback riding. (sad)

5. I'm going to go horseback riding. (angry)

6. I'm going to go horseback riding. (surprised)

Readers' Theater

Directions: Below, you'll find "Horseback Riding" written in play format. Choose one person to play each role. Then, read the piece out loud with the appropriate emotions.

Narrator:	James reread the letter from his cousin with concern.
Bill:	I would like you to visit my ranch. See you soon! From, Bill.
Narrator:	James folded the letter. He wanted to visit, but his mind gave him a preview of what might happen.
	James was afraid of horses. Bill had two. In his head, James saw himself trying to interact with the horses.
James:	But I'm afraid they'll bite me, or throw me to the ground!
Mother:	Go! What you discover might surprise you.
Narrator:	So James went to the ranch.
Bill:	Let me show you my horses. I'll ride one, and you can ride the other.
Narrator:	James felt unhappy. But he walked toward a small black horse.
Bill:	This is Cal. He is a good horse.
Narrator:	Slowly, James climbed into the saddle. He put his feet in the stirrups. He felt at a disadvantage since Bill was an expert rider. But Cal trotted along gently.
Bill:	You're doing fine!
Narrator:	Then, James felt overjoyed. His mother had been right.
James:	I like horseback riding!

Fluency Report Card

Directions: Read the story out loud to your teacher. Ask your teacher to time your reading with a watch.

Together, fill out the chart below.

Rate of Reading	Minutes Seconds
Accuracy	Number of Mistakes
Tone	Pitch, Volume, and Rhythm
What You Did Best	Your strengths in fluency!

Dancing Boy

Jerry wanted to be a dancer. When he was ten, his parents took him to see *The Nutcracker* ballet. Jerry loved the graceful dancers and the beautiful music. "I want to take ballet lessons," he told his parents.

When the kids at school found out that Jerry took ballet lessons, they laughed and laughed. "Dancing is for girls!" they said. "You're a sissy!"

One boy in particular was mean to Jerry. "Dancing Boy! Dancing Boy!" Scotty snickered.

But Jerry kept on with his ballet lessons. In just a few years, he became an expert dancer. "I'll get to dance a lead role in *The Nutcracker!*" he told his mother. "I have to miss school on Friday to give a performance."

What Jerry didn't know is that his entire school would come to see *The Nutcracker*. The house lights went down. The lights on stage went up. They were so bright that he couldn't see who was in the audience. Jerry danced wonderfully that day, leaping and twirling with joy. After the performance, he and other dancers met with people from the audience.

"Jerry, you're wonderful!" Kids from his school crowded around, their faces shining. Then, Scotty walked up with red cheeks. He looked embarrassed. "That was amazing," Scotty said. "Do you think you could teach me how to leap into the air like you do?"

Jerry smiled. "I'd be happy to," he said.

Scotty shook his hand with genuine admiration. "Thank you, Dancing Boy."

True or False

Directions: Study each sentence below. Write *True* or *False* in the space after each sentence.

1. Scotty takes Jerry to see *The Nutcracker* ballet. _____

2. Kids tease Jerry for taking ballet lessons. _____

3. Jerry's parents don't let him take dance classes. _____

4. Jerry is not a very good dancer. _____

5. After Jerry performs, kids look at him with admiration. _____

6. Jerry quits dancing after people make fun of him. _____

7. Scotty has no interest in learning how to dance. _____

8. Jerry refuses to teach Scotty how to leap in the air. _____

Adjectives

An adjective describes a person, place, or thing.

Directions: Study the adjectives from "Dancing Boy" in the Adjective Box below. Then, use each adjective in a sentence. The first one has been done for you.

Adjective Box	
graceful	wonderful
beautiful	embarrassed
expert	amazing
bright	

1. She grew beautiful roses in her garden.

2. _____

3. _____

4. _____

5. _____

6. _____

7. _____

More on Adjectives

Directions: Study the sentences below. Choose an adjective from the Adjective Box that best completes each sentence.

1. The sun was so _____ that they had to wear sunglasses.

2. He performed an _____ trick that involved balancing an egg on his nose.

3. She looked _____ after she tripped and fell in front of the entire class.

4. My cat is a _____ jumper; she always lands on her feet.

5. He is an _____ at math, and he tutors everyone in his class.

6. The girl's painting was so _____ that her mother had it framed and hung it in the living room.

7. "It's _____ that you're learning to play the trumpet!" cried the boy's grandfather.

Adjective Box	
graceful	wonderful
beautiful	embarrassed
expert	amazing
bright	

Inflection

Inflection refers to the emphasis you put on a particular word. You can change the meaning of a sentence depending on which word you emphasize.

Directions: Look at the sentences below. Read each out loud. Give particular emphasis to the word in bold type. Note how the meaning of the sentence changes.

I want to take ballet lessons.

I **want** to take ballet lessons.

I want **to** take ballet lessons.

I want to **take** ballet lessons.

I want to take **ballet** lessons.

I want to take ballet **lessons**.

More on Inflection

Directions: Study the dialogue below from "Dancing Boy." Read it out loud to yourself. Underline those words that you feel should be emphasized. When you are finished, compare notes on inflection with your classmates. The first one has been done for you.

Jerry: I want to take <u>ballet</u> lessons.

Kids: Dancing is for girls!

Scotty: You're a dancing boy.

Jerry: I get to dance a lead role on Friday.

Kids: Jerry, you're wonderful!

Scotty: Do you think you could teach me to dance?

Jerry: I'd be happy to.

Word Search

Directions: Find the words from "Dancing Boy" in the Word Search below. Words may appear up, down, diagonally, forward, and backwards.

l	l	l	e	f	e	z	e
u	u	e	g	a	t	s	d
f	f	f	x	e	a	a	p
r	i	r	e	p	n	t	l
e	t	d	l	c	e	e	r
d	u	r	e	l	a	r	s
n	a	r	l	p	g	r	t
o	e	a	u	p	a	x	g
w	b	m	u	s	i	c	l

Word Bank	
ballet	leap
wonderful	graceful
dancer	expert
beautiful	music

Fluency Report Card

Directions: Read the article out loud to your teacher. Ask your teacher to time your reading with a watch.

Together, fill out the chart below.

Rate of Reading	Minutes Seconds
Accuracy	Number of Mistakes
Tone	Pitch, Volume, and Rhythm
What You Did Best	Your strengths in fluency!

The Bear and the Two Travelers

by Aesop

A fable is a short story that offers a moral. Aesop was an ancient Greek writer who told numerous fables.

Two men were traveling together through the forest. "It's a beautiful day!" said Man One to Man Two. "We'll be at the campground in a few hours."

Man Two smiled. "You're right. We've got a wonderful day for traveling."

Suddenly, a bear jumped in front of them. Man One climbed into a tree and hid himself in the branches. Man Two didn't know what to do. He fell flat on the ground and lay there, terrified.

The bear lumbered up and felt Man Two with his snout. He snuffled in his ear. Man Two couldn't move. He held his breath and pretended to be dead. The bear left then, for it is said that bears won't touch a dead body.

When the bear was gone, Man One jumped down from the tree. "What did the bear say to you?" he asked.

"He gave me this advice," his friend replied. "You shouldn't travel with a friend who leaves you in the face of danger."

Find the Answer

Note: This exercise may be completed in small groups, or with the entire classroom.

Directions: Elect one person to read the first question below. The rest of the group must find the sentence in "The Bear and the Two Travelers" that answers the question. Read the sentence aloud. Then, proceed with the next question.

1. What advice does the bear give to Man Two?

_____

_____

2. Where does Man One hide from the bear?

_____

_____

3. Where are Man One and Man Two going?

_____

_____

4. What does Man One ask Man Two?

_____

_____

5. What does the bear do to Man Two's ear?

_____

_____

6. Why does the bear leave?

_____

_____

7. Does Man Two think it's a good day to travel?

_____

_____

8. Where are Man One and Man Two as this fable begins?

_____

_____

Caption the Picture

Directions: Study the pictures below. Then, write a caption below each picture to explain it. The first one has been done for you.

Man Two and Man One walked through the forest.

_____

_____

_____

_____

_____

_____

_____

_____

_____

_____

Contractions

You can join two words together to make a contraction. Use an apostrophe in place of the letters you leave out.

Directions: Study the words below. Then, read them out loud.

Word	Word	Contraction
it	is	it's
you	are	you're
we	have	we've
did	not	didn't
could	not	couldn't
will	not	won't
should	not	shouldn't

More on Contractions

Directions: Practice writing contractions on your own. Blend each pair of words below to make a contraction. Remember to include an apostrophe in each contraction. Finally, write the letter or letters that you are leaving out of the contraction in the space given. The first one is done for you.

1. should   not   _____shouldn't_____   _____o_____

2. could   not   _____   _____

3. did   not   _____   _____

4. it   is   _____   _____

5. will   not   _____   _____

6. you   are   _____   _____

7. we   have   _____   _____

Contraction Story

Directions: Now that you know how to write contractions, include at least eight from the Contraction Box in a short story. Write your story in the space below.

Contraction Box			
couldn't	won't	it's	we'll
shouldn't	can't	won't	I'll
you're	didn't	he'll	we've

Crossword Puzzle

Directions: Fill in the blanks below and complete the crossword puzzle.

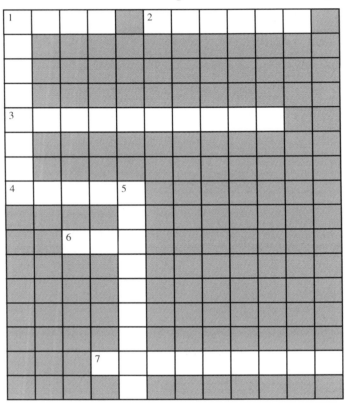

Across

1. A _____ sniffled in Man Two's ear.

2. Man One is not a very brave _____ .

3. Man One and Man Two are traveling to a _____ .

4. The bear felt Man Two with his _____ .

6. The bear said something in Man Two's _____ .

7. Man One thought it was a _____ day.

Down

1. Man One hid in the _____ of a tree.

5. Man Two felt _____ .

Fluency Report Card

Directions: Read the article out loud to your teacher. Ask your teacher to time your reading with a watch.

Together, fill out the chart below.

Rate of Reading	Minutes Seconds
Accuracy	Number of Mistakes
Tone	Pitch, Volume, and Rhythm
What You Did Best	Your strengths in fluency!

Spilled Milk

Read the fable below. What do you think is the moral of the story?

Sarah was the daughter of a farmer. When she turned ten years old, her father called to her.

"Sarah," he said, "It will be your job now to milk our cow and sell the milk at the market. You may have the money you make from the milk."

Sarah felt so excited. The next morning, she woke up at dawn and put on her warm clothes. She walked out to the barn where the cow waited. "Hello, Spot," she said to the cow. "It's milking time."

Spot gave Sarah a pail full of milk. "Thank you," Sarah said, and gave Spot some hay. Then, Sarah carried her pail of milk from the barn to the farmhouse. She began to daydream.

"The money from this milk will buy three hundred eggs," she said. "The eggs will produce two hundred and fifty chickens."

Sarah wrinkled her forehead in thought. "By the end of the year I shall have money to buy a new gown," she exclaimed. "I will go to parties, where all the young men will propose to me, but I will hold up my hand and refuse them every one."

Then, Sarah held up her hand. The movement upset the milk pail, and it fell to the ground. Just like that, all her dreams vanished in a puddle of spilled milk.

Question and Answer

Directions: Answer the questions below in complete sentences.

1. What does Sarah do to upset the milk pail?

_____

_____

2. What does Sarah give Spot in exchange for milk?

_____

_____

3. What will Sarah receive in exchange for her new chore?

_____

_____

4. How many eggs will the pail of milk buy?

_____

_____

5. What does Sarah plan to do with her money?

_____

_____

6. How does Sarah feel when her father asks her to milk the cow?

_____

_____

Order of Events

Directions: Study the sentences below. They describe the fable "Spilled Milk," but they are out of order. Copy the sentences in the proper order of events on the chart at the bottom of the page.

1. Sarah carried her pail of milk from the barn to the farmhouse.
2. Sarah woke up at dawn and put on her warm clothes.
3. The movement upset the milk pail, and it fell to the ground.
4. Then, Sarah held up her hand.
5. Spot gave Sarah a pail full of milk.
6. She walked out to the barn where the cow waited.

1. _____

_____

2. _____

_____

3. _____

_____

4. _____

_____

5. _____

_____

6. _____

_____

Barnyard Bingo

Directions: Copy the words below onto individual file cards or small pieces of paper. Choose one person to be the Caller. The Caller begins by choosing one word to call out. Each player then marks the square on his or her game card which contains that word.

Break into groups of five. Distribute copies of the Bingo cards below and on the next three pages to the other four players. Mark off each word as the caller says it. Players may use markers in the form of dried beans, pennies, or small pebbles. You may want to play so that the first person to mark off an entire row across, down, or diagonally wins. Alternatively, you might want to play until every word has been called and marked.

milk pail	farmhouse	dawn
money	gown	daughter
clothes	puddle	chickens

Barnyard Bingo *(cont.)*

puddle	gown	clothes
daughter	farmhouse	dawn
money	milk pail	chickens

Barnyard Bingo *(cont.)*

daughter	chickens	money
dawn	gown	milk pail
farmhouse	clothes	puddle

Barnyard Bingo *(cont.)*

chickens	clothes	daughter
gown	money	dawn
farmhouse	puddle	milk pail

Fluency Report Card

Directions: Read the article out loud to your teacher. Ask your teacher to time your reading with a watch.

Together, fill out the chart below.

Rate of Reading	Minutes Seconds
Accuracy	Number of Mistakes
Tone	Pitch, Volume, and Rhythm
What You Did Best	Your strengths in fluency!

Fine Feathers

A Peacock and a Crane stood by the river, enjoying the sunset. Over the deep blue water, the sky glowed pink and orange.

"I have never seen anything so beautiful!" exclaimed the Crane.

The Peacock spread out its multicolored tail. "Yes, but it's not as beautiful as I am. I am clothed in gold and purple and all the colors of the rainbow. You are only plain white."

The Crane looked at her own pale feathers. She looked at her long, skinny feet. Then, she gazed at the colorful feathers of the Peacock before her.

"You are correct," she replied gently. "But I can fly high up into the sky, while you can only strut along the dirty ground below."

Then, with a hop and a skip, the Crane flew up toward the pink and orange clouds. The setting sun reflected off her white feathers, turning them golden.

Circling around, she delivered a moral to the Peacock.

"Fine feathers don't make fine birds!"

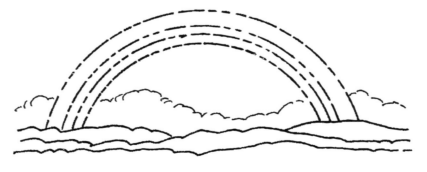

Words and Their Meanings

Directions: Circle the word that best completes each sentence below.

1. In this fable, "glowed" means   **shone**   **firefly**

2. In this fable, "multicolored" means   **pale**   **vivid**

3. In this fable, "strut" means   **walk**   **fly**

4. In this fable, "fine" means   **thin**   **pretty**

5. In this fable, "pale" means   **colorful**   **white**

6. In this fable, "setting" means   **sinking**   **putting**

7. In this fable, "correct" means   **right**   **change**

8. In this fable, "circling" means   **drawing**   **rotating**

Which Adjective for Which Noun?

Directions: Study the pictures on the right side of the page. Study the adjectives on the left. Draw a line from the adjective to the picture it best describes.

blue	
multicolored	
skinny	
pale	
beautiful	
orange	

Label the Pictures

Directions: On each line, write the adjective that best describes the picture to which it is referring. Use the adjectives from the Word Bank below. Then, color the picture.

Word Bank	
skinny	orange
beautiful	pale
colorful	dirty

Flash Cards

Note to Teacher: Make double-sided copies, aligning words with the correct pictures so that they appear front-to-back.

Directions: Cut out these flash cards on the lines. Use them to practice spelling and fluency.

crane	peacock
rainbow	sunset
clouds	feather
ground	river

Flash Cards (cont.)

Emotional Reading

Directions: Read the dialogue from "Fine Feathers" out loud, using the emotion you see in parenthesis after each sentence.

"You are only plain white." (disgusted)

"Fine feathers don't make fine birds." (happy)

"I have never seen anything so beautiful." (excited)

"I am clothed in gold and purple." (proud)

"You are correct." (gentle)

Now, read "Fine Feathers" out loud in Readers' Theater form below. Make sure to add emotion to your reading!

Fine Feathers

Narrator: A Peacock and a Crane stood by the river, enjoying the sunset. Over the deep blue water, the sky glowed pink and orange.

Crane: I have never seen anything so beautiful!

Narrator: The Peacock spread out its multicolored tail.

Peacock: Yes, but it's not as beautiful as I am. I am clothed in gold and purple and all the colors of the rainbow. You are only plain white.

Narrator: The Crane looked at her own pale feathers. She looked at her long, skinny feet. Then, she gazed at the colorful feathers of the Peacock before her.

Crane: You are correct. But I can fly high up into the sky, while you can only strut along the ground below.

Narrator: Then, with a hop and a skip, the Crane flew up toward the pink and orange clouds. The setting sun reflected off her white feathers, turning them golden.

Crane: Fine feathers don't make fine birds!

Fluency Report Card

Directions: Read the article out loud to your teacher. Ask your teacher to time your reading with a watch.

Together, fill out the chart below.

Rate of Reading	Minutes Seconds
Accuracy	Number of Mistakes
Tone	Pitch, Volume, and Rhythm
What You Did Best	Your strengths in fluency!

Writing a Letter

December 10, 2007

Dear Thuy,

How are you? What is the weather like in Vietnam right now?
Here, it is cold and rainy. Tomorrow, we might get two inches
of snow!

I enjoyed my visit with you last summer. The trees are
beautiful where you live. I really liked boating on the river,
too. I will try to make the soup that your mother made for us. I
liked the noodles and the vegetables in spicy broth.

When can you come to visit me in Washington? I would like to
take you hiking in the mountains. My friends want to teach you
how to play baseball, too. Afterwards, we'll take you out for
pizza.

Take care, and I hope to see you soon.

Your friend,

José

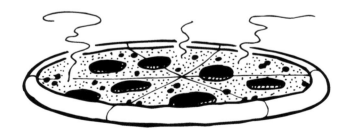

Which Word?

Directions: Study the sentences below. Select the best word to fill in each blank. Write the correct word on the blank.

1. The author of this letter lives in _____ .
   Vietnam   Washington

2. In Vietnam, José went _____ on the river.
   boating   hiking

3. Thuy's mother made a vegetable _____ .
   soup   pizza

4. The _____ is cold and rainy in Washington.
   visit   weather

5. José thinks the trees in Vietnam are _____ .
   beautiful   spicy

6. Thuy is José's _____ .
   mother   friend

7. Tomorrow, Washington might get two inches of _____ .
   rain   snow

8. Over the summer, Thuy and José explored the

   _____ together.
   mountains   river

Word Search

Directions: Find the words from "Writing a Letter" in the Word Search below. Words may be placed vertically, horizontally, diagonally, forward, or backwards.

```
v  w  b  x  c  b  h  i  b  s  g  p  o  y
g  e  f  o  h  g  f  f  n  b  n  s  l  r
g  s  g  a  a  m  u  i  q  v  i  s  m  o
g  s  e  e  s  t  a  h  i  j  k  o  l  n
o  d  y  s  t  t  i  c  h  o  i  u  e  g
p  g  e  c  n  a  w  n  k  b  h  p  q  t
p  i  n  u  b  y  b  b  g  z  x  g  m  d
k  i  o  y  z  l  a  l  r  p  x  y  m  q
x  m  a  c  i  s  f  e  e  r  a  i  n  y
z  c  b  m  e  o  d  c  i  s  n  u  l  e
l  b  s  b  n  o  o  d  l  e  s  n  l  d
m  l  a  a  z  z  i  p  g  m  u  z  j  x
i  l  e  t  f  f  r  i  e  n  d  d  w  n
l  s  n  g  w  h  d  k  l  p  l  c  v  k
```

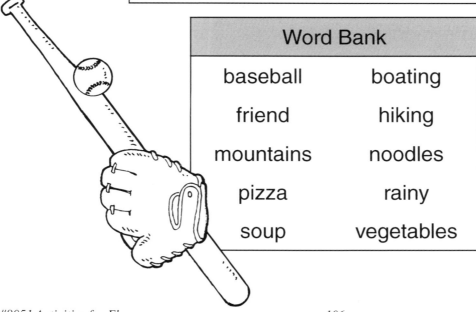

Word Bank

baseball	boating
friend	hiking
mountains	noodles
pizza	rainy
soup	vegetables

Caption the Pictures

Directions: Study the pictures below. Then, write a caption for each picture using words from the Word Bank.

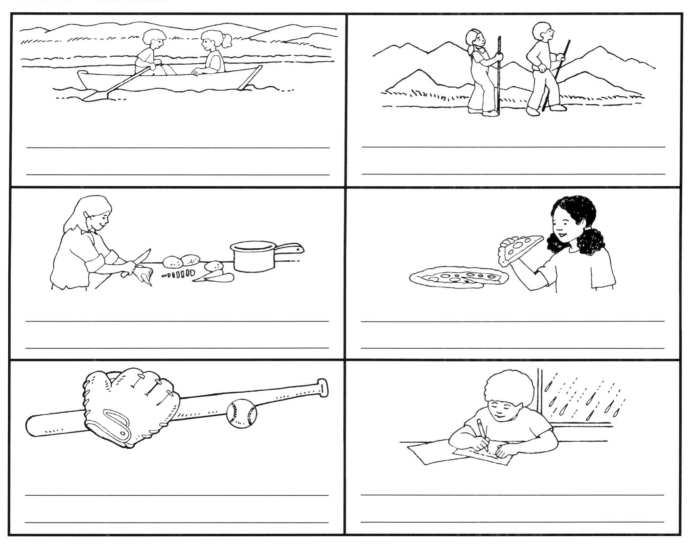

Word Bank		
mountains	river	José
letter	rain	Thuy
pizza	baseball	friend
vegetables	boating	mother

Inflection

Remember that inflection refers to the emphasis you put on a particular word. You can change the meaning of a sentence, depending on which word you emphasize.

Directions: Look at the sentences below. Read each out loud. Give particular emphasis to the word in bold type.

Tomorrow, we might get two inches of snow!
(Not yesterday, and not today.)

Tomorrow, **we** might get two inches of snow!
(We will, but you won't!)

Tomorrow, we **might** get two inches of snow!
(Then again, we might not.)

Tomorrow, we might get **two** inches of snow!
(Not one, but two!)

Tomorrow, we might get two **inches** of snow!
(Not two feet—just two inches.)

Tomorrow, we might get two inches of **snow**!
(Much more exciting than rain.)

Robot Reading

One of the best ways to learn proper inflection is to read incorrectly.

Directions: Break into groups of three. Each of you can take a turn reading the letter below, like a robot. Read in an even, steady tone. Don't let your voice get higher or lower.

December 10, 2007

Dear Thuy,

How are you? What is the weather like in Vietnam right now? Here, it is cold and rainy. Tomorrow, we might get two inches of snow!

I enjoyed my visit with you last summer. The trees are beautiful where you live. I really liked boating on the river, too. I will try to make the soup that your mother made for us. I liked the noodles and the vegetables in spicy broth.

When can you come to visit me in Washington? I would like to take you hiking in the mountains. My friends want to teach you how to play baseball, too. Afterwards, we'll take you out for pizza.

Take care, and I hope to see you soon.

Your friend,

José

When you have finished, answer the questions at the bottom of this page.

Inflection Questions

How does this letter sound when you read like a robot?

_____

_____

_____

How does inflection change the letter?

_____

_____

_____

Your Own Letter

Directions: Write your own letter in the space below. Tell the recipient about your location and your weather. Ask questions of the recipient, as well. Don't forget a date, a greeting, names, and a closing!

When you have finished your letter, read it out loud to your class.

Fluency Report Card

Directions: Read the letter out loud to your teacher. Ask your teacher to time your reading with a watch.

Together, fill out the chart below.

Rate of Reading	Minutes Seconds
Accuracy	Number of Mistakes
Tone	Pitch, Volume, and Rhythm
What You Did Best	Your strengths in fluency!

The Radio Show

Before television, people listened to programs on the radio. Here is a sample script from a radio show.

Host:	Ladies and gentleman, welcome to the Sunny Morning Radio Show. We have a great show planned for you today, with a special guest star.
Duck:	Quack! Quack!
Host:	That's right, folks. Today on our show, we bring you Miss Feathers and her pet duck, Webster!
Miss Feathers:	Thank you for inviting us to be on the show. We're happy to be here, aren't we, Webster?
Duck:	Quack! Quack!
Host:	Is it true, Miss Feathers, that your duck has a special talent that he will share with our listeners today?
Miss Feathers:	Oh, yes, it's quite true. One day, Webster was taking a bath, and I overhead him singing to himself.
Host:	Don't you mean quacking to himself?
Miss Feathers:	No, singing. My pet duck was singing the "Star-Spangled Banner," weren't you, Webster?
Duck:	Quack! Quack!
Host:	That is amazing! Now, Webster, I'm going to put this microphone up close to your bill, and whenever you're ready, please begin singing.

(There is a moment of silence.)

Host:	Um . . . Webster? Is something wrong?
Miss Feathers:	Sometimes he gets shy. I'll sing the first notes. Oh say can you see . . .
Duck:	(quacking in tune with the first line of the "Star-Spangled Banner") Quack-quack quack quack quack quack!
Host:	Absolutely incredible. Thank you, Webster. Thank you, Miss Feathers.
Miss Feathers:	My pleasure.
Duck:	Quack!
Host:	Next on our show, Mr. Furr and his dancing cat! But first, a word from our sponsors.

Question and Answer

Directions: Answer the following questions about "The Radio Show" with complete sentences.

1. What is the duck's special talent?

   _____

   _____

   _____

2. What was the duck doing when Miss Feathers discovered its talent?

   _____

   _____

   _____

3. What song does the duck know how to sing?

   _____

   _____

   _____

4. What is the name of this radio show?

   _____

   _____

   _____

5. Why doesn't the duck sing right away?

   _____

   _____

   _____

6. Following Miss Feather and her duck, who are the guests on the radio show?

   _____

   _____

   _____

Color and Label the Picture

Directions: Color the picture below. Each blank line points to one part of the picture. Label each part, writing words from "The Radio Show" on each line.

True or False

Directions: Answer each question by circling true or false.

1. Miss Feathers is the name of a duck.   **True**   **False**

2. The duck sings words in English.   **True**   **False**

3. Mr. Furr has a dancing cat.   **True**   **False**

4. The radio show is called Sunny Morning.   **True**   **False**

5. The host makes fun of the duck.   **True**   **False**

6. Miss Feathers sings the "Star-Spangled Banner."   **True**   **False**

7. The dancing cat and the singing duck fight.   **True**   **False**

8. The duck quacks into the microphone.   **True**   **False**

Guess the Meaning

Directions: Study the sentences below. Circle the answer which best completes the sentence.

1. In this script, *overheard* means   **sing**   **listen**

2. In this script, *inviting* means   **asking**   **pretty**

3. In this script, *bill* means   **dollar**   **beak**

4. In this script, *pet* means   **stroke**   **loved**

5. In this script, *notes* means   **tune**   **papers**

6. In this script, *great* means   **large**   **fun**

7. In this script, *star* means   **duck**   **sun**

8. In this script, *wrong* means   **hurt**   **problem**

Emotions in Reading

You may have noticed many emotions as you read "The Radio Show" to yourself.

Directions: Study each line below. Then, practice reading it out loud as a class with the emotion you see in parenthesis.

Ladies and gentleman, welcome to the Sunny Morning Radio Show.

(**sleepy**)

We're happy to be here, aren't we, Webster?

(**happy**)

One day, Webster was taking a bath, and I overhead him singing to himself.

(**proud**)

Don't you mean quacking to himself?

(**confused**)

That is amazing!

(**surprised**)

Um . . . Webster? Is something wrong?

(**concerned**)

Absolutely incredible. Thank you, Webster. Thank you, Miss Feathers.

(**amazed**)

Next on our show, Mr. Furr and his dancing cat!

(**enthusiastic**)

Readers' Theater

You can read "The Radio Show" like a play, and even tape record it!

Directions: Choose one person to be the Host. Choose one person to be Miss Feathers. Choose one person to be the Duck. Then, act out the radio show below using inflection and emotions.

Host:	Ladies and gentleman, welcome to the Sunny Morning Radio Show. We have a great show planned for you today, with a special guest star.
Duck:	Quack! Quack!
Host:	That's right, folks. Today on our show, we bring you Miss Feathers and her pet duck, Webster!
Miss Feathers:	Thank you for inviting us to be on the show. We're happy to be here, aren't we, Webster?
Duck:	Quack! Quack!
Host:	Is it true, Miss Feathers, that your duck has a special talent that he will share with our listeners today?
Miss Feathers:	Oh, yes, it's quite true. One day, Webster was taking a bath, and I overhead him singing to himself.
Host:	Don't you mean quacking to himself?
Miss Feathers:	No, singing. My pet duck was singing the "Star-Spangled Banner," weren't you, Webster?
Duck:	Quack! Quack!
Host:	That is amazing! Now, Webster, I'm going to put this microphone up close to your bill, and whenever you're ready, please begin singing.
(There is a moment of silence.)	
Host:	Um . . . Webster? Is something wrong?
Miss Feathers:	Sometimes he gets shy. I'll sing the first note. Oh say can you see . . .
Duck:	(quacking in tune with the first line of the "Star-Spangled Banner") Quack-quack quack quack quack quack!
Host:	Absolutely incredible. Thank you, Webster. Thank you, Miss Feathers.
Miss Feathers:	My pleasure.
Duck:	Quack!
Host:	Next on our show, Mr. Furr and his dancing cat! But first, a word from our sponsors.

Fluency Report Card

Directions: Read the article out loud to your teacher. Ask your teacher to time your reading with a watch.

Together, fill out the chart below.

Rate of Reading	Minutes Seconds
Accuracy	Number of Mistakes
Tone	Pitch, Volume, and Rhythm
What You Did Best	Your strengths in fluency!

The Game Show

Host: Welcome to "What's My Job?" This game show is sure to entertain you. Here's how we play. One employee stands behind this tall screen, hidden from our three players. The players have to guess the employee's job, based on a description. Today, our players are Tran, Sue, and Katy. Are we ready?

All Players: Ready!

Host: Then, let's get started.

Employee #1: Well, I'm always covered in fur, and I smell kind of doggy.

Tran: A dog groomer?

Employee #1: No. Sometimes I have to give small animals a shot or do an operation on them.

Sue: I know! You're a veterinarian.

Host: Congratulations, Sue. You guessed it. Employee #1 is a veterinarian! Here comes employee #2.

Employee #2: I sit in the driver's seat, and I have a lot of passengers.

Tran: My mom?

Employee #2: Sorry, no. My vehicle doesn't travel on roads.

Sue: A railroad conductor?

Employee #2: Guess again! I like sunny skies, free of clouds.

Katy: You're an airline pilot!

Host: Congratulations, Katy. You guessed it! Finally, we've got employee #3.

Employee #3: I do a lot of walking all day, and I meet many friendly people.

Katy: A dog walker?

Employee #3: No, it's just me and my big bag.

Sue: Santa Claus?

Employee #3: Sorry! I make sure your birthday cards get to you on time.

Tran: You're the mail carrier!

Host: Well done, Tran. Well, friends, that's all we have time for today. Thanks for playing "What's My Job?" Each player will receive a special prize for appearing on the show today. See you next week!

Contractions

A contraction is one word which is formed by joining two words with an apostrophe.

Directions: Study the list of words below. Read them out loud. Then, read the contraction from "The Game Show."

what	+	is	=	what's		does	+	not	=	doesn't
that	+	is	=	that's		it	+	is	=	it's
you	+	are	=	you're		we	+	have	=	we've
here	+	is	=	here's		let	+	us	=	let's

Now, it's your turn to make contractions. Look at the words in Box 1. Look at the words in Box 2. Put them together with an apostrophe to form as many contractions as possible in Box 3. You should be able to make at least ten contractions.

Box 1	Box 2
let	are
what	is
it	us
that	have
we	not
does	
you	
here	

Box 3
1. _____
2. _____
3. _____
4. _____
5. _____
6. _____
7. _____
8. _____
9. _____
10. _____

Contractions in Action

Directions: Study the contractions you formed on the previous page. Then, write a letter from one of the players to his or her parents, telling them about the game show. Use at least eight contractions in your letter.

Tools of the Trade

Directions: Study the pictures of three employees. On the line above them, write their job. Then, study the toolkit below. Below each employee, write the names of the tools each might use in his/her job.

Tools:

Tools:

Tools:

Tool Kit

letter

stethoscope

thermometer

syringe

suitcase

package

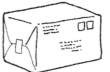

headphones

shoulder bag

sunglasses

Relationships

Directions: Study the relationships below. Fill in the blanks with the correct words. Then, explain the relationship in one sentence. The first one has been done for you.

1. **Cat** is to **veterinarian** as *letter* is to **mail carrier**.

Veterinarians care for cats as mail carriers care for letters.

2. Animals are to veterinarian as _____ are to airline pilot.

_____

_____

3. Players are to game show as _____ are to job.

_____

_____

4. Feet are to mail carrier as airplane is to _____ .

_____

_____

5. Delivering birthday cards is to mail carrier as _____ is to veterinarian.

_____

_____

6. Friendly people are to _____ as sunny skies are to airline pilot.

_____

_____

Crossword Puzzle

Directions: Fill in the blanks below and complete the crossword puzzle.

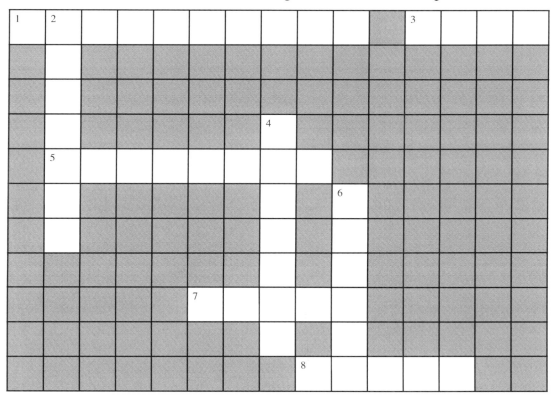

Across

1. Sometimes, veterinarians have to do these.

3. This person makes sure all goes well on a game show.

5. A pilot can't do his job without this.

7. This person takes you safely across the country.

8. This is what you get if you win on a game show.

Down

2. Your mail carrier delivers this to you.

4. These are what veterinarians care for all day.

6. You can send this, thanks to your mail carrier.

Read for Character

You can create a real character when you read, just by adding emotion. Read "The Game Show" out loud, following the description of each character below.

Character	Emotion	Character	Emotion
Host	excited	Employee #2	serious
Employee #1	happy	Katy	shy
Tran	confused	Employee #3	amused
Sue	proud		

Host:	Welcome to "What's My Job?" This game show is sure to entertain you. Here's how we play. One employee stands behind this tall screen, hidden from our three players. The players have to guess the employee's job, based on a description. Today, our players are Tran, Sue, and Katy. Are we ready?
All Players:	Ready!
Host:	Then, let's get started.
Employee #1:	Well, I'm always covered in fur, and I smell kind of doggy.
Tran:	A dog groomer?
Employee #1:	No. Sometimes I have to give small animals a shot or do an operation on them.
Sue:	I know! You're a veterinarian.
Host:	Congratulations, Sue. You guessed it. Employee #1 is a veterinarian! Here comes employee #2.
Employee #2:	I sit in the driver's seat, and I have a lot of passengers.
Tran:	My mom?
Employee #2:	Sorry, no. My vehicle doesn't travel on roads.
Sue:	A railroad conductor?
Employee #2:	Guess again! I like sunny skies, free of clouds.
Katy:	You're an airline pilot!
Host:	Congratulations, Katy. You guessed it! Finally, we've got employee #3.
Employee #3:	I do a lot of walking all day, and I meet many friendly people.
Katy:	A dog walker?
Employee #3:	No, it's just me and my big bag.
Sue:	Santa Claus?
Employee #3:	Sorry! I make sure your birthday cards get to you on time.
Tran:	You're the mail carrier!
Host:	Well done, Tran. Well, friends, that's all we have time for today. Thanks for playing "What's My Job?" Each player will receive a special prize for appearing on the show today. See you next week!

Fluency Report Card

Directions: Read the article out loud to your teacher. Ask your teacher to time your reading with a watch.

Together, fill out the chart below.

Rate of Reading	Minutes Seconds
Accuracy	Number of Mistakes
Tone	Pitch, Volume, and Rhythm
What You Did Best	Your strengths in fluency!

Riddles

Question:
Why do birds fly south?
Answer:
Because it's too far to walk!

Question:
Why do potatoes make good detectives?
Answer:
Because they keep their eyes peeled!

Question:
What do you call a scared dinosaur?
Answer:
A nervous Rex!

Question:
Why was the belt arrested?
Answer:
For holding up the pants.

Question:
Who granted the fish three wishes?
Answer:
The Fairy Cod-Mother!

Flash Cards

Note to Teacher: Make double-sided copies, aligning words with the correct pictures so that they appear front-to-back.

Directions: Cut out these flash cards on the lines. Use them to practice spelling and fluency.

dinosaur	south
fairy	nervous
detectives	potatoes
holding	arrested

Flash Cards (cont.)

Captions

Directions: Study the riddles. Then, study each picture below. Using words from the Word Bank at the bottom of the page, caption each picture.

Word Bank	
south	potatoes
dinosaur	detectives
nervous	arrested
fairy	holding

Word Search

Directions: Find the words from "Riddles" in the Word Search below. Words may be placed vertically, horizontally, diagonally, all facing forward.

```
d e t e c t i v e s z w v d s
h i h j n q m g p l h a y q o
f i n j k l b e x j a r r y u
l t y o t e w y q q i o c u t
b f t e s i t c s a n g w q h
l n x k b a p q f z v c f i t
j e f a g l u o d j u f z o r
e r b m r t e r t h l k f m c
q v p s q r s h g a b o x j m
e o r k c w e n o b t l g i e
w u r s i x b s g l p o e y x
z s k l e h x x t a d d e u k
f p f r x k o m b e k i m s j
a w d v w t w i d m d d n b k
d f o d b y n h e e d u p g i
```

Word Bank

south	dinosaur
nervous	fairy
potatoes	detectives
arrested	holding

Word Relay

Directions: Count off so that you have two teams. Choose team names. On a chalk or dry-erase board, draw two large boxes. Write each team's name over one box.

Ask students to form two lines. Choose someone to be the reader. This person will read aloud from a word list.

After the reader says the first word, the first student on each team will run up to the board and attempt to write the word correctly in that team's box. (If both students write the word incorrectly, the second student on each team comes up to the board to try and write the word.)

The first student to write the word correctly earns a point for his/her team. Repeat with the next student in each line, and a new vocabulary word, until all words have been used.

Congratulate and reward both teams for playing well and learning new words to increase their fluency!

Write Your Own Riddles

Directions: Study the words in Box 1. Study the words in Box 2. Then, combine words from each box to write four riddles of your own!

Box 1
apple
comb
cat
car

Box 2
teeth
tire
core
pause

Riddle 1

Question: _____

Answer: _____

Riddle 2

Question: _____

Answer: _____

Riddle 3

Question: _____

Answer: _____

Riddle 4

Question: _____

Answer: _____

Fluency Report Card

Directions: Read the riddles out loud to your teacher. Ask your teacher to time your reading with a watch.

Together, fill out the chart below.

Rate of Reading	Minutes Seconds
Accuracy	Number of Mistakes
Tone	Pitch, Volume, and Rhythm
What You Did Best	Your strengths in fluency!

Tongue Twisters

Students may practice these classic tongue twisters below and on the next page for a fun method of increasing fluency.

Point out that tongue twisters rely on alliteration—the repetition of particular sounds within a sentence.

While we were walking,
we were watching window washers
wash Washington's
windows with warm washing water.

A flea and a fly flew up in a flue.
Said the flea,"Let us fly!"
Said the fly,"Let us flee!"
So they flew through a flaw in the flue.
A Tudor who tooted a flute
tried to tutor two tooters to toot.
Said the two to their tutor,
"Is it harder to toot
or to tutor two tooters to toot?"
A tree toad loved a she-toad
Who lived up in a tree.
He was a two-toed tree toad
But a three-toed toad was she.

Tongue Twisters *(cont.)*

The two-toed tree toad tried to win

The three-toed she-toad's heart,

For the two-toed tree toad loved the ground

That the three-toed tree toad trod.

But the two-toed tree toad tried in vain.

He couldn't please her whim.

From her tree toad bower

With her three-toed power

The she-toad vetoed him.

Mr. See owned a saw.

And Mr. Soar owned a seesaw.

Now See's saw sawed Soar's seesaw

Before Soar saw See,

Which made Soar sore.

Had Soar seen See's saw

Before See sawed Soar's seesaw,

See's saw would not have sawed Soar's seesaw.

So See's saw sawed Soar's seesaw.

But it was sad to see Soar so sore

Just because See's saw sawed Soar's seesaw!

Award for Accuracy

For reading every word
with skill and accuracy—

with sharp eyes and good
pronunciation, too—

_____

receives this prize!

Award for Rate of Reading

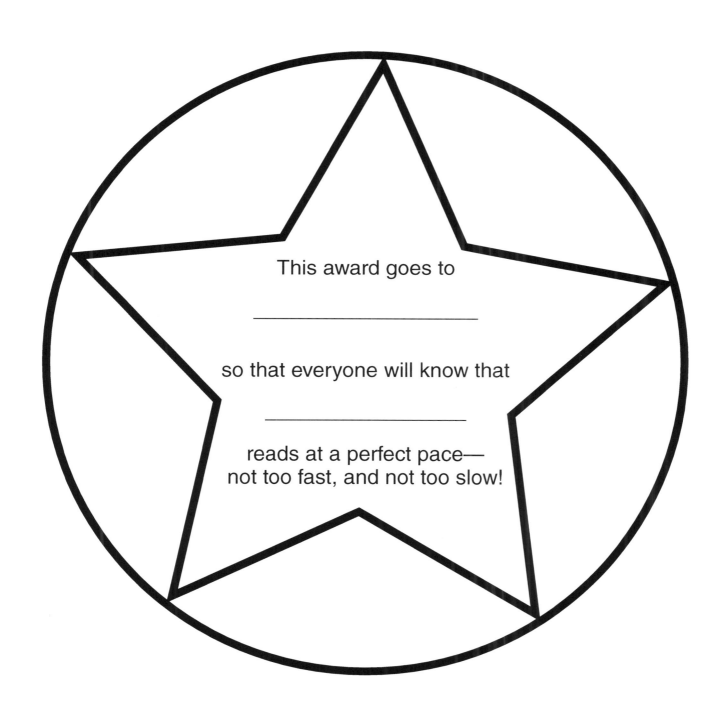

This award goes to

_____

so that everyone will know that

_____

reads at a perfect pace—
not too fast, and not too slow!

Award for Tone

_____

has earned this badge

for tone to please the ear.

Not too high,
and not too loud,

with rhythm that is nice to hear!

Answer Key

Page 11
1. plates
2. buildings
3. Cover
4. earthquake
5. table
6. power lines

Page 12
1. uproot
2. cover
3. power lines
4. plates
5. table
6. earthquake
7. Earth
8. buildings

Page 13
Accept all reasonable captions.

Page 14
Accept all reasonable descriptions.

Page 22
1. aquarium
2. ocean
3. squid
4. blowhole
5. canary
6. Beluga whale

Page 28
Across
1. balloon
2. propane
4. people
6. brothers
7. inflate

Down
1. basket
3. rooster
5. flame

Page 29
Accept all reasonable diary entries.

Page 30
1. False
2. False
3. True
4. True
5. False
6. True

Page 33
1. snow
2. village
3. harness
4. evening
5. farmhouse
6. woods
7. horse
8. snowflake

Page 34
1. one
2. two
3. one
4. two
5. two or three (depending on pronunciation)
6. one

Page 36
1. take
2. lit
3. vil
4. stop
5. prom ses
6. down
7. love
8. be

Page 37
1. house
2. ness
3. mis
4. sy
5. zen
6. mi
7. est
8. be

Page 38
Accept all reasonable answers.

Page 51

k	i	n	g	b	d	i
n	i	o	s	i	n	g
b	m	s	q	r	m	d
r	a	e	u	d	o	i
e	i	d	e	n	n	s
a	d	r	e	e	e	h
d	a	i	n	t	y	e

Page 52
Accept all reasonable answers which use given words.

Page 54
1. The queen and the king like to eat pie and cookies.☺ Sometimes they like to eat cake.☺
2. I love to wake up in the morning to hear the birds singing.☺ It puts me in a happy mood.☺
3. Where is that blackbird going?☺ He is flying very close to that woman's nose!☺
4. I love to count my quarters and dimes.☺ Then, I take them to the store and buy candy.☺
5. Bees make honey.☺ Do you like to eat your bread with honey, peanut butter, or jam?☺
6. When you hang your clothes on the line to dry, they smell like fresh air.☺ But watch out for birds.☺

Page 57
Accept all reasonable definitions.

Page 58
1. lucky
2. excitement
3. sadly

4. hopeless
5. sledding

Accept all reasonable definitions.

Page 59

lucky
luckless
openly
opener
opening
sadly
sadder
sledder
sledding
player
playful
playing
hoper
hopeful
hoped
hopeless
excited
excitement
wisher
wished
wishing

Page 60

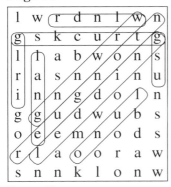

Page 62

Accept all reasonable sentences.

Page 65

Accept all reasonable definitions.

Page 66

1. reread
2. discover
3. unhappy
4. disadvantage

5. interact

Accept all reasonable definitions.

Page 67

1. preview
2. unhappy
3. disadvantage
4. interact
5. reread
6. overjoyed
7. discover
8. remarkable

Page 68

Accept all reasonable captions.

Page 73

1. False
2. True
3. False
4. False
5. True
6. False
7. False
8. False

Page 74

Accept all reasonable sentences.

Page 75

1. bright
2. amazing or expert
3. embarrassed
4. graceful
5. expert
6. beautiful
7. wonderful

Page 78

Page 81

1. "You shouldn't travel with a

friend who leaves you in the face of danger."
2. Man One climbed into a tree and hid himself in the branches.
3. "We'll be at the campground in a few hours."
4. "What did the bear say to you?" he asked.
5. He snuffled in his ear.
6. The bear left then, for it is said that bears won't touch a dead body.
7. We've got a wonderful day for traveling."
8. Two men were traveling together through the forest.

Page 82

Accept all reasonable captions.

Page 84

1. shouldn't   o
2. couldn't   o
3. didn't   o
4. it's   i
5. won't   ill, o
6. you're   a
7. we've   ha

Page 86

Across

1. bear   6. ear
2. friend   7. beautiful
3. campground
4. snout

Down

1. branches
5. terrified

Page 89

1. Sarah waves her hand, which causes the milk pail to fall.
2. Sarah gives Spot hay in exchange for the milk.
3. Sarah will receive money from selling the milk.
4. The pail of milk will buy 300 eggs.

5. Sarah plans to buy a new gown with the money.
6. Sarah feels excited when her father asks her to milk the cow.

Page 90

1. Sarah woke up at dawn and put on her warm clothes.
2. She walked out to the barn where the cow waited.
3. Spot gave Sarah a pail full of milk.
4. Sarah carried her pail of milk from the barn to the farmhouse.
5. Then, Sarah held up her hand.
6. The movement upset the milk pail, and it fell to the ground.

Page 97

1. shone
2. vivid
3. walk
4. pretty
5. white
6. sinking
7. right
8. rotating

Page 105

1. Washington
2. boating
3. soup
4. weather
5. beautiful
6. friend
7. snow
8. river

Page 106

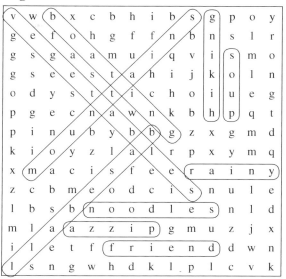

Page 107

Accept all reasonable captions that use words from the Word Bank.

Page 110

Make sure students include date, greeting, closing, and names, along with place and weather details.

Page 113

1. The duck's special talent is quacking the tune to the first line of the "Star-Spangled Banner."
2. The duck was taking a bath when Miss Feathers discovered its talent.
3. The duck knows how to "sing" the "Star-Spangled Banner."
4. The name of this radio show is the "Sunny Morning Radio Show."
5. The duck doesn't sing right away because it is shy.
6. Following Miss Feather and her duck, Mr. Furr and his dancing cat are the guests on the radio show.

Page 115

1. False
2. False
3. True
4. True
5. False
6. True
7. False
8. True

Page 116

1. listen
2. asking
3. beak
4. loved
5. tune
6. fun
7. duck
8. problem

Page 121

1. let's
2. what's
3. it's
4. that's
5. we're
6. we've
7. doesn't
8. you're
9. you've
10. here's

Page 122

Accept all reasonable letters.

Page 123

Veterinarian—stethoscope, syringe, thermometer
Airline pilot—suitcase, headphones, sunglasses
Mail Carrier—shoulder bag, letter, package (Sunglasses is an acceptable answer here, as well.)

Page 124

2. passengers
3. employees
4. pilot
5. operating
6. mail carriers

Page 125

Across

1. operations
3. host
5. airplane
7. pilot
8. prize

Down

2. package
4. animals
6. letter

Page 131

Accept all reasonable captions.

Page 132

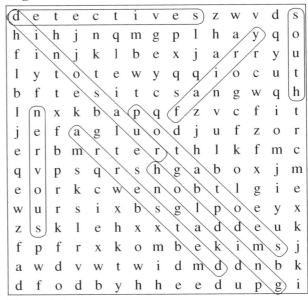

Page 134

Accept all reasonable riddles.

Made in United States
Orlando, FL
21 January 2022